Roll away
the boring stuff!

in Excel 365 and 2021

Ina Koys

Short & Spicy, vol. 13

Contents

0	What we're going to talk about	1
1	Input habits and shortcuts	3
2	Data types	9
3	Built-in lists	17
4	Create your own lists	23
5	The benefits of the table functionality	29
	5.1 Matters of beauty	29
	5.2 Calculations	37
	5.3 Filtered lists	42
6	Establishing good relations	45
7	The icing on the cake: Quadrangular results	51
8	Flash Fill	55
9	The Quick Access Toolbar	61
10	More	65

0 What we're going to talk about

Many users need to perform the same steps over and over again. In many cases, these works can be left to Excel. It will do it quicker, without typos and won't ever complain about repetitive work. We will see how to save manual typing, how to keep Excel from doing what it better should leave, how to set correct cell references and make lists convenient to use.

All screenshots are done in Excel 365, but most of the features presented here, work exactly the same in all Excel versions, only sometimes with a slightly different look.

If you'd like to download the example files, you can do so clicking

www.shortandspicy.online

Have fun shifting your work to Excel from now on!

What we're going to talk about

1 Input habits and shortcuts

Of course, you can jump to any Excel cell as you like: using your mouse, the cursor keys, or the keyboard. But getting used to certain standard procedures you can avoid unnecessary adjusting.

First of all, I would suggest working your way in reading direction using the **TAB** key. It's the one with the two arrows on the left of your keyboard. Each single time pressing it advances the cell cursor one column to the right. Doing it this way supports the normal reading and writing direction if you need to fill in the data yourself. That's not too special so far. The real advantage begins once you reached the end of your row and want to continue at the beginning of the next row. If you now hit **ENTER**, your cell cursor jumps right below the cell you first pressed **TAB**.

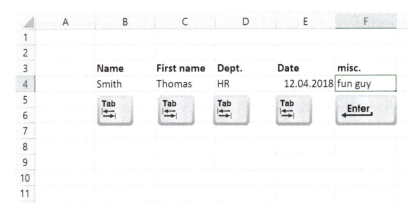

Then, you can go on with the next name without fiddling around with your mouse pointer. Because if you have a lot to write, it will always interrupt the flow and needlessly costs you time you may want to use a better way.

Apart from that, the **TAB** key also works the other way round: the upper arrow on the key is activated exactly the same way all double keys are operated: using the **SHIFT** key. Then, it will work itself down the way to the right.

Now talking about the **ENTER** key we may have a look at the many other purposes it can serve. Normally, hitting the key will bring you to the cell just below – if you didn't reach your current cell using the **TAB** key. But sometimes, you do not want that. Sometimes, you simply want to complete you cell entries and then maybe format them. To get this done, hold down the **CTRL** key and then hit **ENTER**. You now stay in the cell you are and can keep doing things there. And as we are talking about shortcuts: **SHIFT** and **ENTER** will bring you to the cell above the one you're in.

The **CTRL** key also has another function that may delight very attentive users – rather scatter-brained ones may regret using it. Because sometimes you may like to make the same entry in the same cell of different sheets. To get this done, hold down the **CTRL** key and activate all sheets that should receive this entry and write your text or formula. Then, hitting **ENTER**, this entry will get written in all the cells in all the sheets activated. But do take care! If there was a former content you were not aware of and in fact wanted to keep, it'll be bad luck. There won't be a further inquiry or warning. The entry will be in for all sheets activated and the effect remains as long as they remain activated.

Input habits and shortcuts

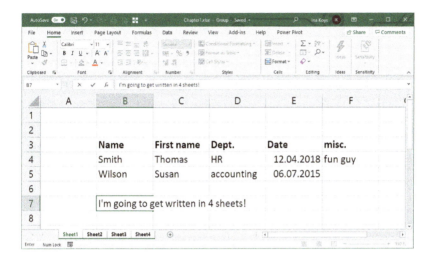

To deactivate the sheets, it does to click any other sheet name. And if you notice that something is messed up, there is still a chance to hit **CTRL + Z** to undo your deeds. Still, if the background saving is done (normally every 10 minutes), that will be too late. Therefore, in case of any doubt, better be cautious.

Now talking about habits, you may re-think your wording. Where there are fixed expressions, the matter is clear, and they have to be written. No doubt about that. But sometimes it's about decisions that can be made one or the other way. Then, one has some freedom to make different decisions. Still, in case of Excel do not take this freedom! Because a rather uniform working habit can make your work much more efficient than inspiration.

Let's take an example from real life. A list of construction defects needs to be written from recording. A specialist walked the rooms and dictated what was noticed.

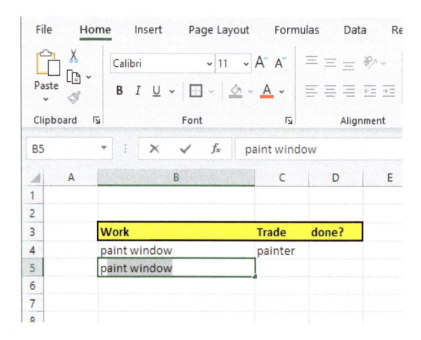

As soon as Excel believes to have understood what you're intending to type, it will suggest that content. If it fits, press **TAB** or **ENTER** (depending on your desired work direction) to have it inserted. If it does not fit, simply keep typing. In the next cell with text content, the game begins anew. Especially with extensive content and using uniform expressions especially at the beginning of a cell you may save a lot of typing!

The automatic completion of a cell ends with any empty row. So, if you really need empty rows in a sheet, insert them later. It can be done i.e., using your **right** mouse button. And do take the chance to

Input habits and shortcuts

check the other entries in the context menu. For many normal functions like cell formatting, you may be quicker beginning here than via the **Start** tab, where they are of course also provided.

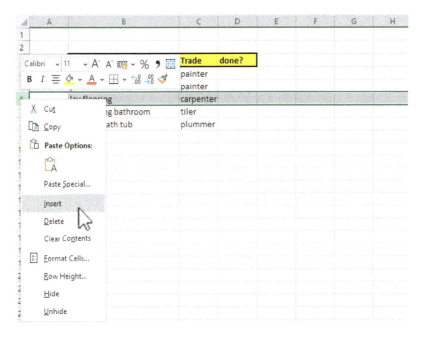

At the beginning of this chapter, we already talked about shortcuts. There are in fact so many of them, that a list of them can be stretched across many pages. Hardly anybody uses them all. Whether you like them or not is mostly a matter of taste. Still, I'd like to recommend some of them, as they are useful and can be used pretty often.

Across all of Windows you can use:

CTRL + C......Copy marked item to the clipboard

Input habits and shortcuts

CTRL + X ..... Cut out the marked item

CTRL + V ..... Paste content from the clipboard to cursor position

CTRL + A ..... Highlight all content

CTRL + Z ...... Undo last action

CTRL + N ..... New item in respective environment. In Excel that would be a new workbook.

CTRL + P ...... Open print dialogue

CTRL + S ...... Save

CTRL + F ...... Find / open search dialogue

CTRL + O ..... Open file

And finally, you may enjoy a function key: hitting **F12** on the top right of your keyboard opens the **Save as…** dialogue.

A shortcut much enjoyed and specific to Excel is **CTRL + ;**. It will write the current date into the active cell.

If you enjoy shortcuts, do keep an eye on your mouse pointer. In most cases while hovering a button, it displays a reminder which shortcut alternatively would do the job.

2 Data types

Often, people don't type their data in manually. Instead, it's imported from SAP or other external applications. You then may encounter phenomena that initially appear strange but can be explained taking a closer look. Excel uses numerous data types. That means, numerals and texts are treated differently. Most of the times, this will make sense in the respective context. But if not, it can easily be detected and fixed. Let's have a look at an example:

	A	B	C	D
1				
2				
3	12345 $	12.35	23/10/2020	I am text!
4				
5				
6				

Here, I typed some data in a new, empty sheet. And one thing is obvious: text is handled differently than numbers. Numbers are aligned to the right margin, texts to the left one. Apparently, also the date is a number. Keep that in mind if strange phenomena occur. In case of any doubt, have a look at the **Home** tab.

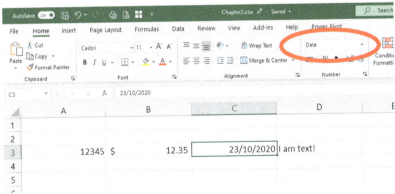

Data types

The date is recognized as **Date** here. Now set the time forth by 1000 years and then back by 200 years.

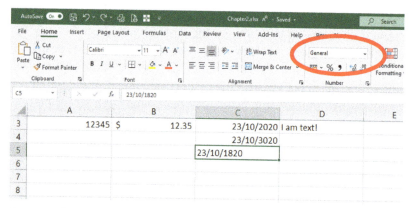

Apparently, something is wrong with the date of 200 years ago. It looks like it is no date at all – contrary to the counterpart in the future. The future one even gives me the full name of the month.

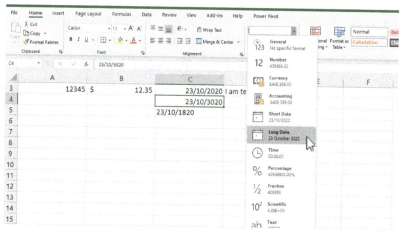

Less convenient is, that in the respective cell of 23/10/1820, I only see a garden fence after selecting the **Long Date**.

Data types

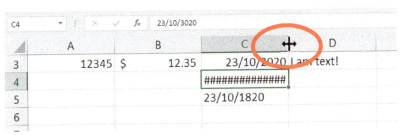

I now drag the outer margin of the column with the left mouse button held down. Performing a double click on the right margin, the column normally finds the room it needs to all on its own. But the date formatting does not work for the date of eighteen-something. To further explore this, I type a '1' into one cell and have it displayed as date. Doing this, I will see the first day after creation of the world - according to the beliefs of Excel.

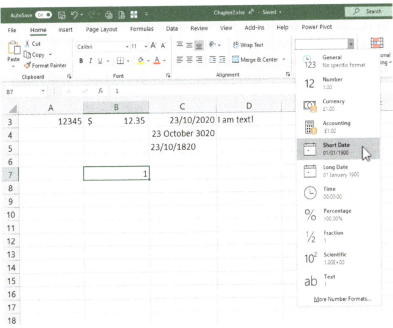

11

Data types

Now I see that Excel is sure the world was created at the beginning of January 1st, 1900. Before that, nothing existed and therefore, no previous date is possible, either. Any date or time is counted from that moment on. It also explains why you normally can't display negative times, if specifying a time only. There was nothing before the beginning of time and therefore, nothing can be calculated. So, if you need negative times, type them in together with a date or turn back the time via **File / Options**.

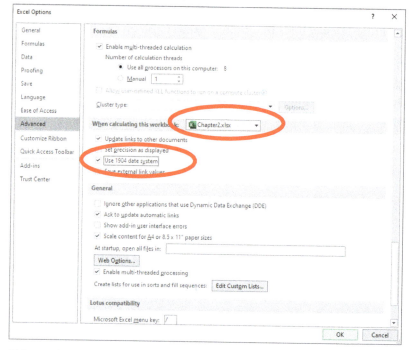

This setting can cause interesting results, therefore keep in mind it's only applied to the current workbook, but here, across all sheets. It can result in the change of data values already used! In case of any doubt, rather leave everything the way it was:

Data types

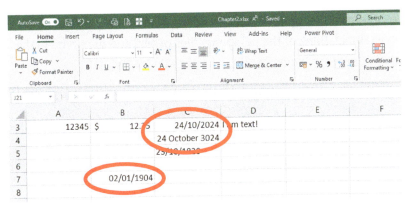

Sometimes and for sometimes unclear reasons Excel displays a simple user input or the result of a calculation as date. Maybe instead of '65' it displays a date of the year 1900 (or 1904, if you changed the setting, too). But by now it's clear, it's a simple matter of formatting. We can adapt it to what we prefer using the formatting drop-down. Internally, Excel anyway uses binary or decimal numbers. Dates, fractions, currencies, and others are only user preferences Excel readily displays for our convenience but does not use itself.

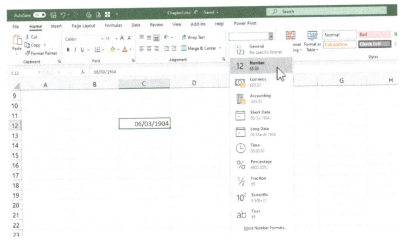

Another thrilling chapter is the handling of apparent numbers. For an example, think of the personnel files of MI6 and then type in the staff number of James Bond:

	A	B	C	D
16				
17				
18	Bond:	007		
19	Smith:			
20				

Hitting the **ENTER** button he lost his double-O prefix and probably along with it the permission to kill.

	A	B	C	D
16				
17				
18	Bond:	7		
19	Smith:			
20				
21				

The explanation is simple: Excel tries to make sense of our entries and finds that in a number, pre-set 0's are pointless. Therefore, it drops them. But the numbers used here, aren't meant to be numbers: you do not want to sum up the personnel numbers of your agents or intend to find an average value of them. Therefore, make them text. Previously omitted 00's won't return after that, but from now on, will remain in any cell that is formatted as **text**.

Data types

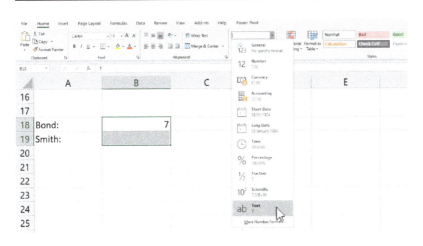

If you now apply a personnel number to agent Smith, he will retain it the way you typed it in. And after hitting **ENTER**, the cell also shows a green corner. Hovering it with your mouse pointer, it'll tell you the reason: it's text now and therefore, calculations with formulas are not possible anymore.

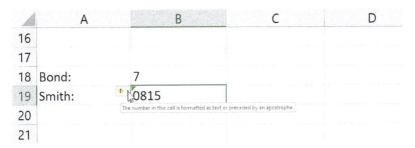

But that's what we wanted. And also the standard alignment in the cell provides the respective feedback: texts stick to the left margin as long as I don't change it manually, i.e. using the buttons in the **Home** tab.

Data types

3 Built-in lists

Some useful lists are already provided in Excel. Just in case you don't know them yet, let's have a closer look at them.

Hovering the bottom right corner of the active cell with your mouse pointer, the arrow changes to a black cross.

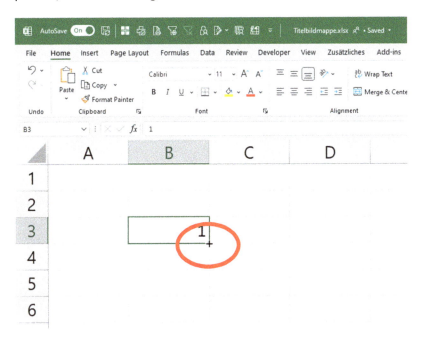

If you now hold down the left mouse button and drag down, the content of the cell gets copied to these cells. Releasing the mouse button, you also get a **SmartTag** next the marked area, offering possibilities you may prefer, just in case you're not completely happy with the offer made by Excel.

Built-in lists

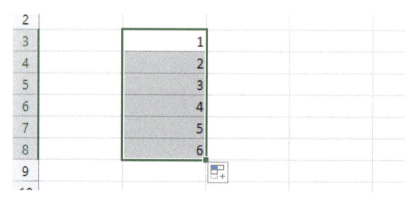

If you i.e., intend to count, select **Fill Series**.

Alternatively, it can be useful to copy content without formatting or, to the contrary, to copy the formatting and leave the previous content as is.

Built-in lists

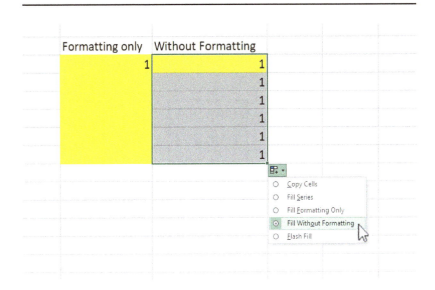

If you're interested in **Flash Fill**: it's been granted a whole extra chapter. Here, we'd better have a look at what other complements Excel has to offer. For example, Excel can detect desired increments. To get it done, type and highlight the first three entries and then drag down.

The effect will also work with complimentary text entries.

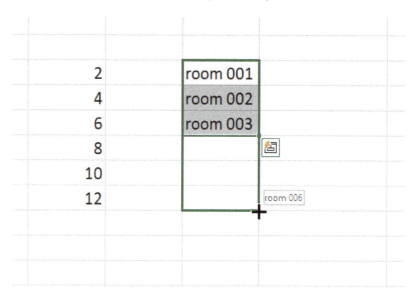

Likewise, also the days of the week and month names will be understood and incremented.

20				
21	Jan	January	Mon	Monday
22	Feb	February	Tue	Tuesday
23	Mar	March	Wed	Wednesday
24	Apr	April	Thu	Thursday
25	May	May	Fri	Friday
26	Jun	June	Sat	Saturday
27				

And by the way: you don't need to include the weekend in your listing. In case you only want to see working days here, opt for **Fill Weekdays**.

20				
21	Jan	January	Mon	Monday
22	Feb	February	Tue	Tuesday
23	Mar	March	Wed	Wednesday
24	Apr	April	Thu	Thursday
25	May	May	Fri	Friday
26	Jun	June	Sat	Monday
27				
28				○ Copy Cells
29				○ Fill Series
30				○ Fill Formatting Only
31				○ Fill Without Formatting
32				○ Fill Days
33				⊙ Fill Weekdays
				○ Flash Fill

The Fill Weekdays function will also work with dates. Dragging them down, make your decision whether to include week-ends or not.

These possibilities may make you dream of what it could be like to have lists of your own here, automatically filling in your custom entries. It is possible and we are going to cover that in the next chapter.

Built-in lists

4 Create your own lists

Often enough, one needs to use similar lists in different contexts. Maybe this time, you need to do a list of customer requests regarding articles, next time it's orders or customer complaints. Always regarding products of the same suppliers. If you have the lists on the same sheet, you can of course simply copy them. But alternatively, you can store them now and forever in Excel to have them conveniently at hand. This feature exists since long, but nowadays is well hidden. We'll get hold of it anyway. It is in the **Backstage Area** (yes, that's its official name!). Therefore, go to *File / Options / Advanced* and scroll down to the **General** part. There, you'll find **Edit Custom Lists…**. Click the button.

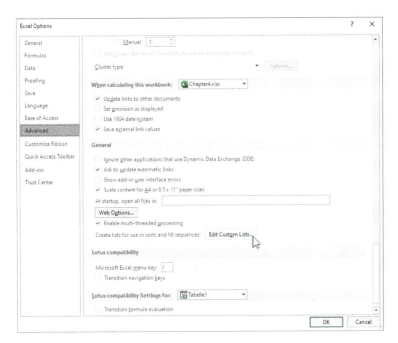

Create your own lists

Now you see the explanation why Excel knows days and months – anyway in English, maybe in other installed languages, too.

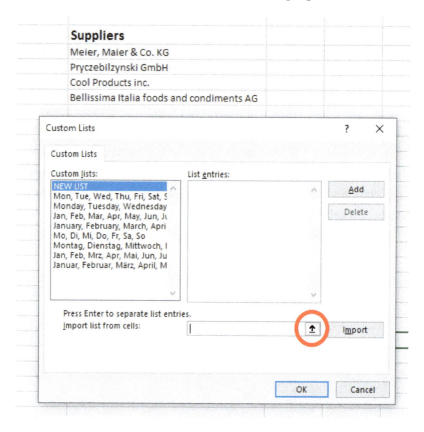

Please note the cursor already set in the input field on the bottom. This field has a symbol on the right you should watch out for and appreciate. It can save you needless typing and appears frequently in Excel dialogues. It signalizes you can simply click outside the window and mark the desired entries with your mouse. After highlighting

Create your own lists

the respective content, they will be transferred to the form without you bothering for the details.

To look at the process here in detail, make sure the cursor is already in the input field. If so, you can safely click outside the window and highlight the prepared list in the sheet. Doing that, the dialogue window will fold down to minimum size...

... and unfolds again as soon as you release the left mouse button.

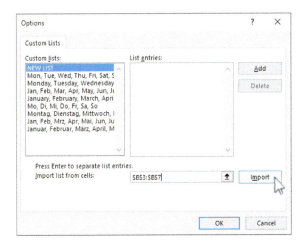

I here included the list title as this one is clearly the shortest entry here. I'll show you in a minute why I did this. Anyway, a click on **Import** sends the marked entries to the above part of the window.

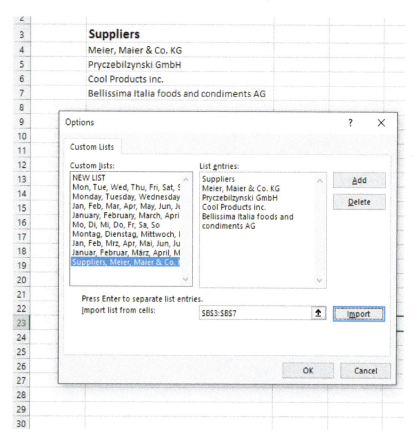

Two clicks on **OK** later, you are back on your worksheet and can check the outcome of your work. Just write any entry of your list correctly into a cell – I will definitely take the uppermost one for being most convenient to write. Then click **ENTER** and go back to your

Create your own lists

input cell. Alternatively, put **CTRL + ENTER**, so your entries are finalized without sending the cell cursor somewhere else. Then, again drag down the bottom right corner of the cell.

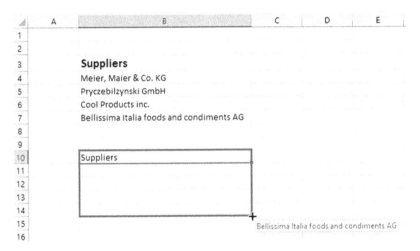

Now, release the mouse button.

Indeed, you don't need to drag down, you can do it to any of the four sides.

After a while, it may well be you need to change something about the list. Then you go back to *File / Options / Advanced* and the **General** section, activate the desired list and change the entries in the window on the right. If you need a new one, click behind the preceding entry and hit **ENTER**.

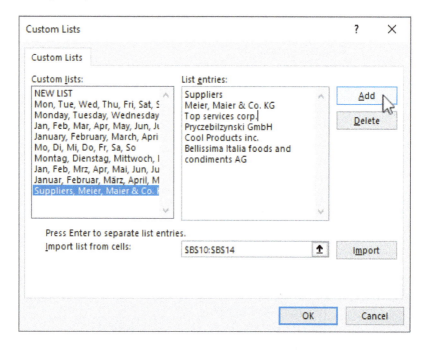

Do make sure that after any changes, you hit **Add**. Only after that, your changes will be saved.

5 The benefits of the table functionality

You may think Excel consists of tables. But that's not thoroughly correct: Excel consists of workbooks containing sheets and sheets containing cells. But between the sheets and the cells one may create another category, the tables. At first sight, it can appear as if they were a bunch of formats and only a matter of taste. If so, I wouldn't grand them a whole chapter. Indeed, there's a lot more about them that can make your Excel life much easier.

In general, the data to be converted to a table needs to meet certain requirements to unfold all its benefits:

o   They need to have a simple structure: same number of rows and columns. That means to abstain from merged or split cells vertically or horizontally.

o   Headers are restricted to no or only one row.

o   If you can, no empty rows, as they would contradict the idea of the tables.

5.1 Matters of beauty

If a range of data meets the requirements, simply click somewhere in the desired range, and select from the **Home** tab, in the **Styles** section, **Format as Table**. (please note that depending on your window size, that tab section may look slightly different from the following picture!)

The benefits of the table functionality

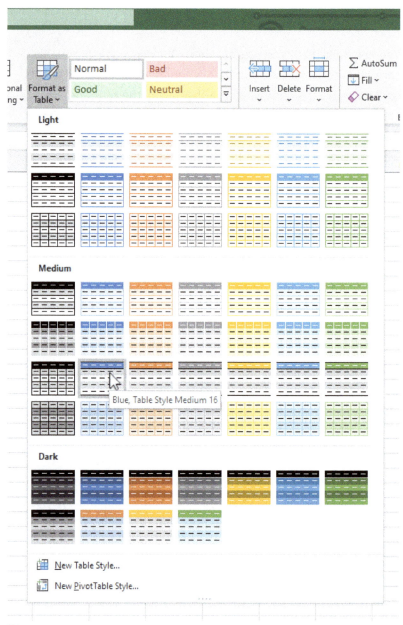

You now get this choice of numerous different formattings. By and large, they all offer the same features, but not all equally clearly visible. Thus, now select one of the styles from **Medium 15** to **Medium 21** where it works best. If you later want to set up your own style for tables, you can do so using **New Table Style...** on the bottom of the choice. Still, it seldom will be worthwhile.

For our example, I put **Blue, Table Style Medium 16**. After clicking it, Excel tries to make sure the correct data range is detected.

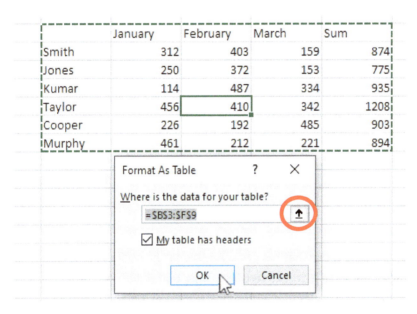

In case of any misdetections, you now can adjust the area with your left mouse button held down (the concept of the arrow symbol in the input field is already mentioned in Chapter 4). Sometimes, you may want to uncheck the header entry. Anyway, then hitting **OK** the range of cells becomes a table and is formatted as desired.

The benefits of the table functionality

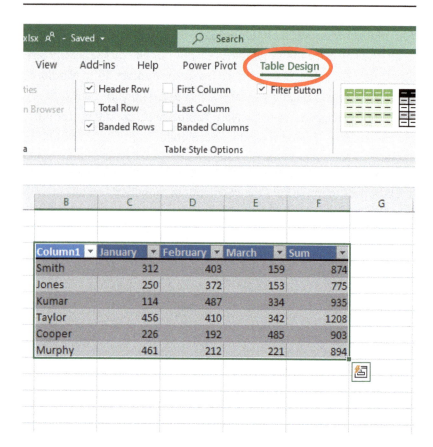

But there's more that happens. Additionally, you'll get one more tab, a so-called 'context-sensitive' one, that only is displayed if the corresponding element – here, the table – exists and is clicked. Sometimes, you may have performed some other tasks in the other tabs and the **Table Design** tab is hidden by other tabs you will have to click it in order to have it activated and displayed on top of the other tabs.

The benefits of the table functionality

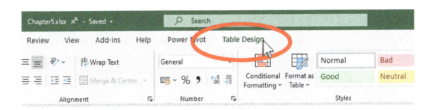

Now having our **Table Design** tab in front, let's have a look around. The table has acquired the selected formatting. Still, there might be details that would do well with improvement. Here, I dragged the A column much wider, so all interesting features get visible here.

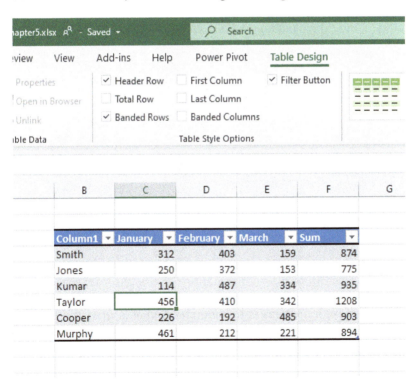

The benefits of the table functionality

The colouring of the tabs differs slightly between this and previous Excel versions, but the features provided are the same. This is only a small example table but do think of one of these often huge specimen you have in real life making it too easy to lose track. Keep the cell cursor within the table and scroll down. You will see the table header merging with column letters.

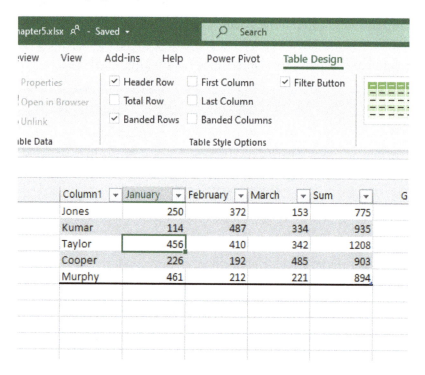

This will make it a lot easier to understand what is what in the table. It also explains why you won't succeed to keep the cell on top of the names empty. There always needs to be an unambiguous content in here. Otherwise, Excel will insert something on its own. Still, if you really don't want to see anything in there, you may put blanks with your space bar. This will be unambiguous, too. I now inserted it here.

Now scroll back to the top again and let's have a look at the different **Table Style Options**. In a table like this, it will certainly be useful to bring out the first and last column. You'll get it done with two mouse clicks.

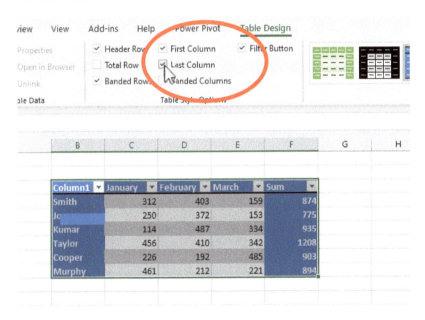

After that, there is more overview already. Let's focus now on the grey and white bands in the background of the table. They are very useful in the wide tables one often has in real life. There, it can be tricky to understand which data belongs together. Now with these bands, you can forget about the grid optics that is not yet fully extinct. And the best part: these bands care for themselves! If you insert new rows or delete them, the bands will always remain correct.

The benefits of the table functionality

If you still want to get rid of them, simply uncheck **Banded Rows**. And maybe also try checking **Banded columns**.

Two more interesting features can be found in the **Table Style Options**, too. The **Header Row** checkbox hides or displays an existing header while **Total Row** adds it row. We'll be taking a closer look at it in the Filter section. I use it most of the times.

Now maybe check out the different **Table Styles** offered on the right of the **Table Design** tab. Go with your mouse across the different sets. Thanks to Live Preview you can observe the different looks of your table without even clicking them. And if you enjoy the table function we are going to cover in the next part, but not the colours, and would prefer a rather basic look, also this solution is offered.

You will seldom need to switch off the table function. But if you intend to do so anyway, it can be done here in **Table Design** clicking **Convert to Range**. The feature will keep data and formatting but set back the calculation and filter settings to what would work even without the table.

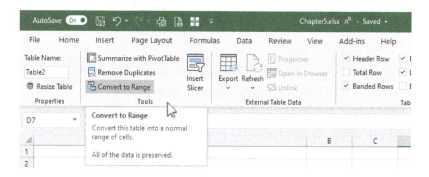

5.2 Calculations

The beauty features of the table are a matter of personal taste. But using the calculations offered you could be able to save samey works by the score. To demonstrate that, I copied a part of the table to a new sheet. I now will perform a very simple calculation. It will do for an example, but in fact, it could be as complex as you want. If you in real live already have an empty column, it of course would work, too. But let's have a look at what happens if you write something next to an existing table.

To demonstrate the effect, I wrote "double January" in **D3** and hit the **ENTER** button.

	A	B	C	D	E
1					
2					
3			January	double J	
4			Smith	312	
5			Jones	250	
6			Kumar	114	
7			Taylor	456	
8			Cooper	226	
9			Murphy	461	
10					

After that, a whole column is added to the table. If I did not want this, I could undo it using the flash symbol next cell **D4**. And I should adjust the column width to make the long text fit in.

The benefits of the table functionality

Now it's getting interesting: Into cell **D4** I write a calculation to double the value of **C4**. I don't type it, I only begin with **=**, click the **C4** with the mouse pointer and then multiply by **2**.

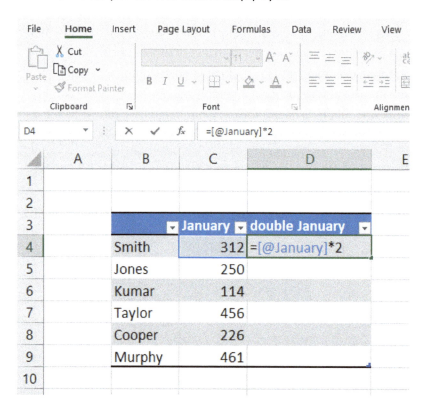

This makes already clear that the display of calculations in a table differs from what is used traditionally. I really like it as I find it easier to understand. Still, you don't need to keep it like this. If you prefer using normal cell relations, you can still do it like that. All the following effects will also work with them. To display the first of them, now hit the **ENTER** button.

The benefits of the table functionality

	A	B	C	D	E
1					
2					
3			January	double January	
4		Smith	312	624	
5		Jones	250	500	
6		Kumar	114	228	
7		Taylor	456	912	
8		Cooper	226	452	
9		Murphy	461	922	
10					
11					

Now all cells in this column perform the same calculation, right down to the bottom. And if you need to change something about the calculation, it works best if you again do it in the first cell. It will then be copied to all other ones. This can save you lots of work fiddling around with the relations. We are going to cover them anyway in more detail in chapter 6.

Some very common calculations can be done even easier using the **Quick Analysis** tool which in this context probably develops its greatest charm. It is an again improved version of the **SmartTag**, which can facilitate the work in many ways. Still, it is not yet used as widely as it deserves.

It is always displayed once the whole table is highlighted. This can be done using your mouse or, alternatively, clicking any cell within the table and then pressing **CTRL** and **A**. Now the whole table is

The benefits of the table functionality

highlighted and in the bottom right corner you'll find the **Quick Analysis** symbol.

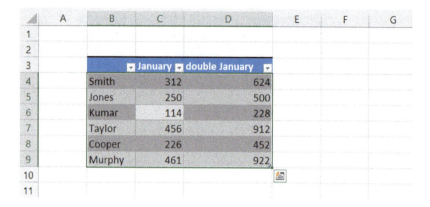

Now click the symbol or hit **CTRL** + **Q** to unfold it.

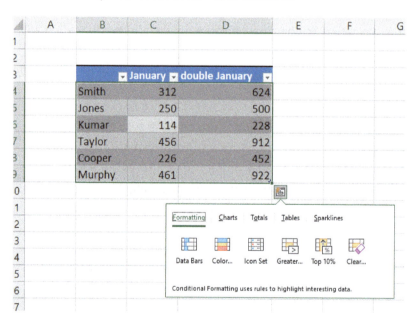

The benefits of the table functionality

This **Quick Analysis** tool offers several pretty different features. Here, we're only interested in what's provided in the **Totals** tab.

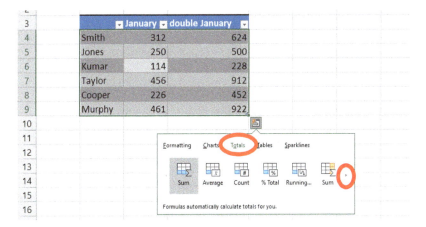

Hover the options with your mouse. Also check out what's hiding on the right of the tab. It's the same totals for rows or columns.

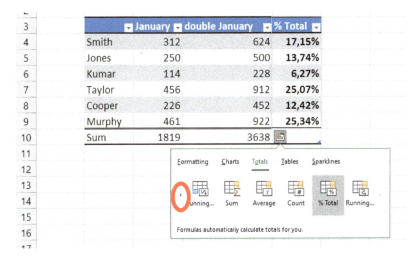

It's hard to see how standard calculations can be made any easier. And do notice the **Running Total**: doing this manually would be much more hassle!

5.3   Filtered lists

At least equally nice will be the outcome of working with the **Filter**. We are not going to explain all the details of the feature here, that deserves a chapter of its own. Just in case you don't know it yet: using the arrow symbol you can filter entries in a list or table.

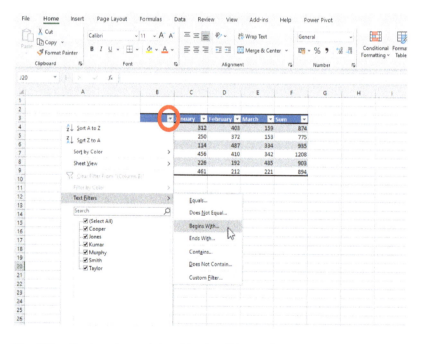

The Filter feature is explained in detail in my booklet 'Queries, VLookup, XLookup & Co.' of this series.

The benefits of the table functionality

Back to the table features, now adjust the style of your example table as you like. But do make sure you activate the **Total Row**.

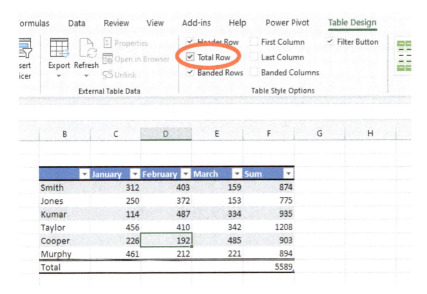

Excel kindly put one total below the **Sum** column – but what kind of total is it? It will tell me after clicking the arrow next the cell.

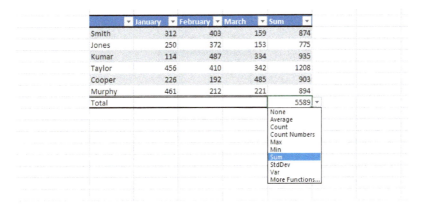

The benefits of the table functionality

With this dropdown, most of the commonly desired calculations can be performed with a mouse click. The same features are offered in any cell of the **Total Row**, even if they make most sense used in columns with numbers. And of course: you can change the label in the first cell from the general **Total** to anything you prefer.

And finally, the icing of the cake comes when changing your filter criteria. I now set the filter to display only Jones and Murphy. The result of the **Total Row** is and will always remain correct. Such a convenient handling of filter results only comes with the table feature.

B	C	D	E	F
	January ▼	February ▼	March ▼	Sum ▼
Jones	250	372	153	775
Murphy	461	212	221	894
Max	461 ▼	372 ▼	221	894

```
None
Average
Count
Count Numbers
Max
Min
Sum
StdDev
Var
More Functions...
```

6 Establishing good relations

By now, we did come across several relations in table cells without spending any attention. So far, they have not had to be explained. Excel always puts them correctly. But now, we did reach a point to explain them in detail. They are of fundamental importance for calculations in Excel.

Let's have a look at a little example using **SUM()** – the best known function throughout Excel. After activating the cell right below a column, one only needs to click the **Σ**-symbol that can be found i.e. on the right in the **Home** tab

	A	B	C	D	E	F
1						
2						
3		10	15	20		
4		20	30	40		
5		30	45	80		
6		40	60	160		
7		100	150	300		
8		=SUM(B3:B7)				
9		SUM(**number1**, [number2], ...)				
10						

The **SUM()** function is automatically inserted and most of the times, the correct range of cells is suggested. Hitting **ENTER** you confirm the suggestion for the current cell. If we now want to perform the same operation for all the other columns, too, we don't need to begin from scratch. It absolutely does to drag the bottom right corner of the cell with the left mouse button held down. Excel will understand it's supposed to sum up the values in the (here) 5 cells

45

above. That's widely known and works the same also for rows and calculations.

	A	B	C	D	E
1					
2					
3		10	15	20	
4		20	30	40	
5		30	45	80	
6		40	60	160	
7		100	150	300	
8		200	300	600	
9					
10					
11					

This very easy task will fail if you attempt to calculate with constants. In our example, we'd like to find the gross price using the net price and VAT.

	A	B	C	D	E	F	G
10							
11							
12		VAT		20%			
13							
14		net	gross				
15		£ 100.00	=B15+B15*C12				
16		£ 200.00					
17		£ 300.00					
18		£ 400.00					
19		£ 500.00					
20		£ 600.00					
21		£ 700.00					
22							
23							

Hitting **ENTER**, the gross price of £ 120.00 will correctly be calculated. But then dragging down the bottom right corner of **C15** as we did accordingly in the previous example, the result turns out somewhat strange.

12	VAT	20%
14	net	gross
15	£ 100.00	£ 120.00
16	£ 200.00	£ 200.00
17	£ 300.00	#VALUE!
18	£ 400.00	£ 48,400.00
19	£ 500.00	£ 100,500.00
20	£ 600.00	#VALUE!
21	£ 700.00	£ 33,880,700.00

It can't be correct that way. But why is that? To explore the reason, double-click i.e., cell **C17**, that apparently does not want to calculate at all.

	A	B	C	D	E	F
12		VAT		20%		
14		net	gross			
15		£ 100.00	£ 120.00			
16		£ 200.00	£ 200.00			
17		£ 300.00	=B17+B17*C14			
18		£ 400.00	£ 48,400.00			
19		£ 500.00	£ 100,500.00			
20		£ 600.00	#VALUE!			
21		£ 700.00	£ 33,880,700.00			

Like before, the cells included in the calculation are set off with a different colour. I now can understand that the attempt to multiply 300 £ by the word 'gross' is bound to fail. Why does Excel try to do that? Because by default, it memorizes cell positions relatively to the current cell. In the case of cell **C15** with the £ 120, it's understood internally as "I have to multiply the cell on my left by the one 3 rows above me and then I have to add again the one on my left". In **C15**, this makes sense and can be done. But in all others below, its results are partly nonsense, partly impossible. Now what we need is a way to make Excel understand the importance of cell **C12** with the VAT percentage. This can be done using the **$**-symbol we already have seen several times. This dollar sign is always added before the part of the cell relation that is meant to be fixed.

- **C12 – relative relation**
  If you drag a cell using this relation, the relation to cell C12 will be dragged likewise to different cells.

- **C12 – absolute relation**
  If you drag a cell using this relation, all other cells will use the value of C12.

- **$C12 – fixed column**
  Dragging the cell corner, the relation will anyway remain in the C column.

- **C$12 – fixed row**
  Dragging the cell corner, the relation will anyway remain in row 12.

Pretty often, in real life there are two meaningful options to adjust the cell relation. In our example, this would be the second and fourth option of this little list. Dragging down, I won't face the risk to slip out of the column. Therefore, I can fix it, but don't need to. Only the **$** symbol before the row reference is important. I now correct the calculation in **C15**, drag down and now get the desired, meaningful results.

	A	B	C	D	E
10					
11					
12		VAT		20%	
13					
14		net	gross		
15		£ 100.00	£ 120.00		
16		£ 200.00	£ 240.00		
17		£ 300.00	£ 360.00		
18		£ 400.00	£ 480.00		
19		£ 500.00	£ 600.00		
20		£ 600.00	£ 720.00		
21		£ 700.00	£ 840.00		
22					
23					

If you find the positioning of the **$** symbol with your mouse too tricky, have a look at your keyboard. You will find the **$** sign sharing the key with **4**. That is a good aid to remind you that alternatively, have the **F4** key to be used to switch between the different relations. After placing the cursor in a relation, each time hitting **F4** will toggle between the different possibilities.

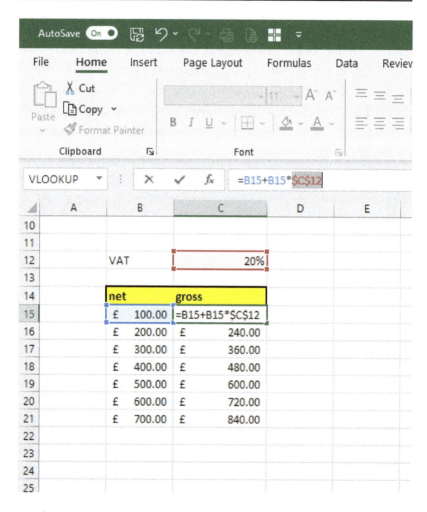

Maybe there are topics in this booklet you do not need. But awareness and appropriate use of correct relations is the key to any mildly advanced use of Excel. Wherever you see relations, you can change them, if you need. And sometimes, like here, only the correction of the default version will deliver a reasonable result.

7 Close to witchcraft: Quadrangular results

Using appropriate relations, you can achieve a lot. But sometimes, you may want even more. Imagine you need to calculate areas. Maybe it must be done very quickly on the telephone. In such a case, you don't have time to type with one hand into the calculator or an Excel sheet, you simply want to read it from a table at your fingertip. If you plan to create such a sheet only with relation, this will turn out to be a joyless task. You may have to create or adjust a whole lot of calculations. But in fact, you only want to multiply ranges of different lengths and widths. You would certainly wish for an easier way to get it done. It does, and here comes the trick. The longer your range of data is, the clearer the advantage of the following procedure. Only to make it printable here, I again created a small table again.

	A	B	C	D	E	F	G	H	I	J	K	L	M
1													
2		length in m											
3													
4			0.1	0.2	0.3	0.4	0.5	0.6	0.7	0.8	0.9		
5		0.1											
6		0.2											
7		0.3											
8	width in m	0.4											
9		0.5											
10		0.6											
11		0.7											
12		0.8											
13		0.9											
14													

Close to witchcraft: Quadrangular results

I now highlight all the cells in the table which I want to assign the calculated area to, beginning in C5. Then, I put = and mark all the cells of the first range I want to include in the calculation.

	A	B	C	D	E	F	G	H	I	J	K	L
1												
2		length in m										
3												
4			0.1	0.2	0.3	0.4	0.5	0.6	0.7	0.8	0.9	
5			0.1	=C4:K4								
6			0.2									
7			0.3									

Now, I press * for the multiplication and highlight the measures of width.

B5   ✗ ✓ fx   =C4:K4*B5:B13

	A	B	C	D	E	F	G	H	I	J	K	L
1												
2		length in m										
3												
4			0.1	0.2	0.3	0.4	0.5	0.6	0.7	0.8	0.9	
5			0.1	=C4:K4*B5:B13								
6			0.2									
7			0.3									
8		width in m	0.4									
9			0.5									
10			0.6									
11			0.7									
12			0.8									
13			0.9									

Close to witchcraft: Quadrangular results

Now, hit **ENTER** and be done!

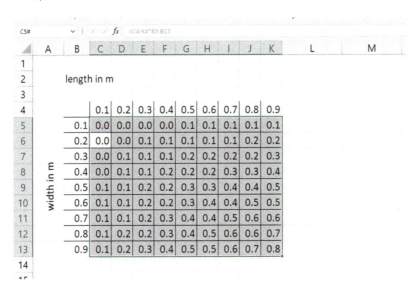

All the cells now contain the correctly calculated results. In this example it is not instantly visible as only one decimal place is displayed. To get the second one, too, click the corresponding icon in the **Home** tab.

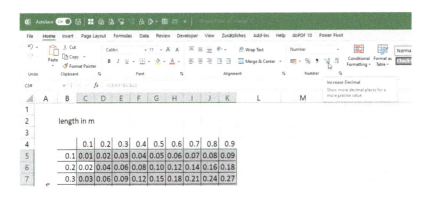

Close to witchcraft: Quadrangular results

After that, I see meaningful results for the square metres in all the cells and I only needed to create one equation to achieve that.

	A	B	C	D	E	F	G	H	I	J	K
1											
2			length in m								
3											
4				0.1	0.2	0.3	0.4	0.5	0.6	0.7	0.8	0.9
5			0.1	0.01	0.02	0.03	0.04	0.05	0.06	0.07	0.08	0.09
6			0.2	0.02	0.04	0.06	0.08	0.10	0.12	0.14	0.16	0.18
7			0.3	0.03	0.06	0.09	0.12	0.15	0.18	0.21	0.24	0.27
8		width in m	0.4	0.04	0.08	0.12	0.16	0.20	0.24	0.28	0.32	0.36
9			0.5	0.05	0.10	0.15	0.20	0.25	0.30	0.35	0.40	0.45
10			0.6	0.06	0.12	0.18	0.24	0.30	0.36	0.42	0.48	0.54
11			0.7	0.07	0.14	0.21	0.28	0.35	0.42	0.49	0.56	0.63
12			0.8	0.08	0.16	0.24	0.32	0.40	0.48	0.56	0.64	0.72
13			0.9	0.09	0.18	0.27	0.36	0.45	0.54	0.63	0.72	0.81
14												
15												

Do notice, that it works that easy only in current versions of Excel! Previously, one needed a special shortcut to get it done. If working with anything up to Excel 2019, one needs to press **CTRL + SHIFT + ENTER** to enter the correct calculation for all the cells.

8 Flash Fill

Many people must deal with lists. Maybe to analyse results per entry, or as data base for mail merge. Pretty often, these lists are not fully in the right shape for the purpose. They are exported from an application by a different person who may not be aware of special requirements. For long, the only way to deal with that was manual correction or text functions. That works but can take up a lot of time. If you have tasks like this, you will love the **Flash Fill**.

Again, we have a little example. It contains UK addresses which are somewhat shortened only for better display here.

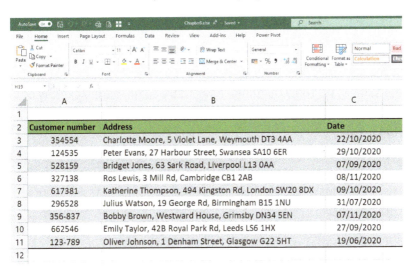

From this table, I would first like to extract the family names. To make it work, it's important to use a column next to the existing data. Leave no column empty as this would impede the feature. You can insert it later if you need.

Flash Fill

Alright. I wanted to extract the family names and write the first one into **D3**. Then I go to the cell below and begin to type the Mr. Evans' name.

	A	B	C	D
1				
2	Customer number	Address	Date	
3	354255	Charlotte Moore, 5 Violet Lane, Weymouth DT3 4AA	22/10/2020	Moore
4	124535	Peter Evans, 27 Harbour Street, Swansea SA10 6ER	29/10/2020	Evans
5	528159	Bridget Jones, 63 Sark Road, Liverpool L13 0AA	07/09/2020	Jones
6	327138	Ros Lewis, 3 Mill Rd, Cambridge CB1 2AB	08/11/2020	Lewis
7	617281	Katherine Thompson, 494 Kingston Rd, London SW20 8DX	09/10/2020	Thompson
8	296528	Julius Watson, 19 George Rd, Birmingham B15 1NU	31/07/2020	Watson
9	356-837	Bobby Brown, Westward House, Grimsby DN34 5EN	07/11/2020	Brown
10	662546	Emily Taylor, 42B Royal Park Rd, Leeds LS6 1HX	27/09/2020	Taylor
11	123-789	Oliver Johnson, 1 Denham Street, Glasgow G22 5HT	19/06/2020	Johnson
12				

Now I only need to press **ENTER** and all entries up to the millionth cell are correctly detected and put in. This feature can save a lot of work but is somewhat delicate. If you don't hit **ENTER** early enough or maybe turn down the suggestions, you may not get this list again the same way. You would then have to try again in the next row or find the well-hidden button for the **Flash Fill** on the right of your **Home Tab**.

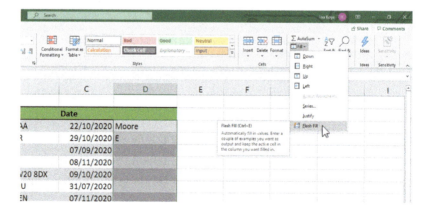

56

Flash Fill

There, you will also get the hint which shortcut you may like to use: **CTRL + E**. If you feel you may not remember it forever, relax. In the last chapter we'll have a look at ways how to place hidden features somewhat handier.

If you anyway now see the list of names on your sheet, simply check out what happens if you attempt to extract different parts of your data record. It will work smoothly for most of the times. But maybe not always. Excel pretends to be smart, still, it's not. Or not as much as claimed. One often understands why it does what, but sometimes, it leaves us clueless. Still, it can be corrected anyway. I added to more rows to the table to clarify the effect.

Have a look at the customer numbers. Their structure differs, maybe due to the merge of different data bases. The first ones are regarded as numbers. Therefore, Excel is reluctant to simply repeat them. So, after writing in the first one (watch out for typos!), just encourage it by highlighting column **D** and hitting **CTRL + E**.

Customer number	Address	Date	
354554	Charlotte Moore, 5 Violet Lane, Weymouth DT3 4AA	22/10/2020	354554
124535	Peter Evans, 27 Harbour Street, Swansea SA10 6ER	29/10/2020	124535
528159	Bridget Jones, 63 Sark Road, Liverpool L13 0AA	07/09/2020	528159
327138	Ros Lewis, 3 Mill Rd, Cambridge CB1 2AB	08/11/2020	327138
617381	Katherine Thompson, 494 Kingston Rd, London SW20 8DX	09/10/2020	617381
296528	Julius Watson, 19 George Rd, Birmingham B15 1NU	31/07/2020	296528
356-837	Bobby Brown, Westward House, Grimsby DN34 5EN	07/11/2020	356-837
662546	Emily Taylor, 42B Royal Park Rd, Leeds LS6 1HX	27/09/2020	662546
123-789	Oliver Johnson, 1 Denham Street, Glasgow G22 5HT	19/06/2020	123-789
	Katherine Thompson, 494 Kingston Rd, London SW20 8DX	09/10/2020	617381
957945	first new data set	07/10/2020	957945
289-934	second new data set	13/04/2020	289-934

Flash Fill

You should now see clearer that 3 data sets contain a dash, maybe from that different data base. We want to get rid of them and make it all look nice and even.

Normally, all we need to do is to remove the misconception or error where it first occurs. It would be Brown in our example. I remove the dash, hit **ENTER** and get a weird result.

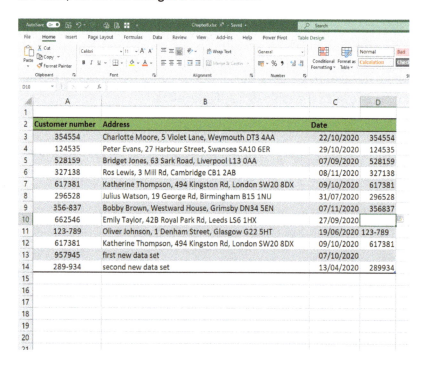

Excel does not tell me why it believes I want to see something like this. Now I could spend ages to find the reason or simply correct the outcome by again typing the correct result beginning from the first misconception. We are getting there.

Flash Fill

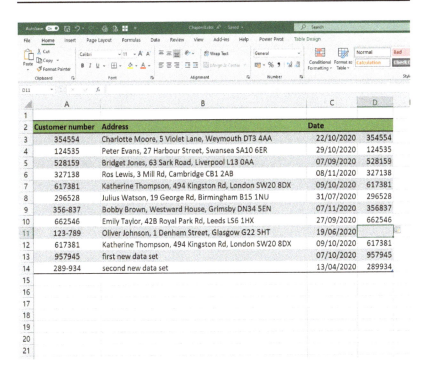

For some reason, the second new data set is corrected, only Johnson now has a blank. Correcting this one, too, will get it right.

This was an exceptionally long process to adjust the **Flash Fill** to our intentions. In fact, I haven't seen such hassle before, it occurred when creating this example and I could not find out what the problem is. Still, it makes pretty clear that the process is a black box, but strictly working top down, it will understand. And don't forget: this will work for thousands of rows!

Likewise, you can also change the structure of your data or change capitalization.

Flash Fill

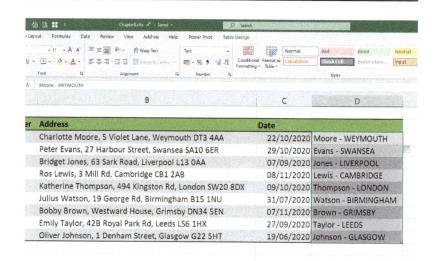

The same way, you may add a comma after the town names or a country name at the end of the data set. Possibilities are plenty. But be careful handling dates and numbers. Sometimes, you may find less than obvious changes. Better double-check to make sure nothing's getting messed up.

9 The Quick Access Toolbar

Right now, we had a good example with the **Flash Fill**. Some features are really well hidden, some others exist since ages, but never made it to the standard interface. But maybe you would love to have them at hand instead of searching the ribbons time and again for what you need for your work. If such a button is already somewhere in the ribbon, this is an easy task to complete. Click it with your right mouse button and select **Add to Quick Access Toolbar**.

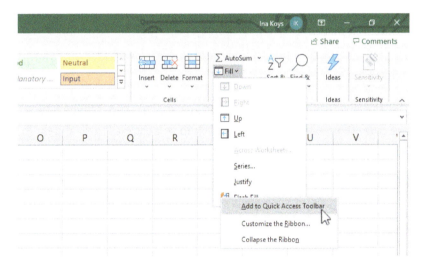

After that, you'll find the button exactly there on the top left of ribbon, where Microsoft by default only puts a small selection of features: **Save**, **Undo** and **Redo**, in Excel 365 also **AutoSave**.

The Quick Access Toolbar

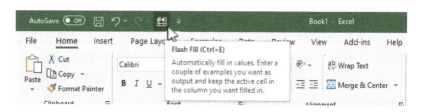

Here, as in many different places, you can get a reminder of possible shortcuts, when hovering the button with your mouse pointer.

But let's keep working with the **Quick Access Toolbar** itself. It can be the start to find many other features that otherwise are difficult or impossible to find. You won't need many of them for your work, but some can help you a lot. To find them, click the little arrow on the right of the toolbar.

The already displayed standard features are checked. Maybe you like something else out of the list. When you click it, it will appear in your **Quick Access Toolbar**. I enjoy i.e. the **Print Preview and Print**.

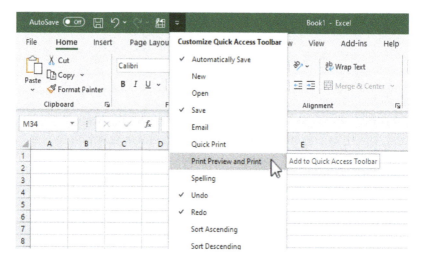

Maybe you miss different features, too, which are not displayed here. To get hold of them, click **More Commands...** on the bottom of the **Custumize Quick Access Bar** dropdown. It will take you to a window that contains an incredible lot, but initially will only offer a reduced choice of features. All of them will only be accessible by unfolding the **Choice of commands** and picking **All Commands**. Simply double-click a command to move it from the choice to right side. Everything there will appear in that order in your bar. If you want to sort them a different way, use the arrows on the left. There is no right or wrong here, only stuff you like and stuff you don't. Just check it out – if you don't need something, you can always throw it out again, i.e., using this window again.

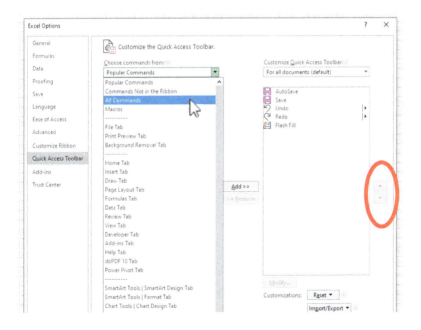

The Quick Access Toolbar

10 More

The **Short and Spicy** series is available on several platforms. Currently, we have these volumes:

Vol. 1:	Outlook as your personal assistant (Outlook 2010-2016)
Vol. 2:	Office 2019 – what's new?
Vol. 3:	Office 365 – What's new?
Vol. 4:	The Digital Notebook
Vol. 7:	Roll away the boring stuff!
Vol. 9:	How to avoid mistakes
Vol. 10:	Text Processing for students
Vol. 11:	Queries, VLookup, XLookup & Co. (full colour)
Vol. 12:	How to create Explainer videos (full colour)
Vol. 13:	Roll away the boring stuff! (full colour)
Vol. 14:	How to get instant overview (full colour)
Vol. 15:	Outlook 365 as your personal assistant (full colour)

... these and all new ones on www.shortandspicy.online!

Also available on Espresso Book Machine!

CPSIA information can be obtained
at www.ICGtesting.com
Printed in the USA
BVHW092131060522
636309BV00003B/153